fun·tastic

Conversation Starters

for **parents & kids**

by Robert C. Crosby

Honor Books
Tulsa, Oklahoma

To Pamela, my soul mate and
partner in parenting.
How I thank God
for the question I asked
and the answer you gave.

Additional copies of this book and other titles by Honor Books
in partnership with Focus on the Family®
are available from your local bookstore.

Also available in this series:
Creative Conversation Starters for Couples

If you have enjoyed this book, or if it has
impacted your life, we would like to hear from you.
Please contact us at:

Honor Books
Department E
P.O. Box 55388
Tulsa, Oklahoma 74137
Or by e-mail at info@honorbooks.com

FOCUS ON THE FAMILY®

Welcome to the Family!

It began in 1977 with the vision of Dr. James Dobson, a licensed psychologist and author of best selling books on marriage, parenting, and family. Alarmed by the many pressures threatening the American family, he founded Focus on the Family, now an international organization dedicated to preserving family values through the life-changing message of Jesus Christ.

For more information about the ministry, or if we can be of help to your family, simply write to Focus on the Family, Colorado Springs, CO 80995 or call 1-800-A-FAMILY. Friends in Canada may write to Focus on the Family, P.O. Box 9800, Stn. Terminal, Vancouver, B.C. V6B 4G3 or call 1-800-661-9800. Visit our Web site at www.family.org.

We'd love to hear from you!

fun·tastic

Conversation Starters

Great questions to ask—

Your Preschooler:

What is a church?

Your Grade-schooler:

What is one thing of yours you would
never be willing to sell at any price?

Your Teenager:

Are there any questions you
would like to ask me?

fun·tastic Conversation Starters

Great questions to ask—

Your Preschooler:
When do you think you'll be old enough
to drive a car?

❖

Your Grade-schooler:
If you could be the President of the United
States for one day, what would you do?

❖

Your Teenager:
Is God your friend?

Conversation Starters

Great questions to ask—

Your Preschooler:
Who is your favorite person in the Bible?

Your Grade-schooler:
What do you think you were like as a baby?

Your Teenager:
What does it mean to be a good steward
of your money and possessions?

fun·tastic

Conversation Starters

Great questions to ask—

Your Preschooler:
What is the newest word you've learned?

Your Grade-schooler:
What is wisdom, and how do you get it?

Your Teenager:
Why are athletes paid more money than policemen or teachers?

fun·tastic Conversation Starters

Great questions to ask—

Your Preschooler:

What are some games that boys and girls both like to play?

Your Grade-schooler:

What is your earliest memory as a kid?

Your Teenager:

What are some of the best things happening in our world today?

Conversation Starters

Great questions to ask—

Your Preschooler:
Why was baby Jesus born in a stable?

❖

Your Grade-schooler:
How do you think Jesus talked to kids
when He lived on earth?

❖

Your Teenager:
What are your five favorite books?

fun·tastic

Conversation Starters

Great questions to ask—

Your Preschooler:
Do you sometimes like to be all by yourself?

Your Grade-schooler:
How do you think God feels about you?

Your Teenager:
How do you know when God is leading you to do something?

fun·tastic Conversation Starters

Great questions to ask—

Your Preschooler:

What story would you like me to read to you?

Your Grade-schooler:

What kind of relationship do you have
with Jesus?

Your Teenager:

What do you think is the most interesting
part of the Bible?

Conversation Starters

Great questions to ask—

Your Preschooler:
Would you sing your favorite song for me?

Your Grade-schooler:
If you could only have one picture of our family, which one would it be?

Your Teenager:
What do you like the most about growing older?

fun·tastic

Conversation Starters

Great questions to ask—

Your Preschooler:

How did you get to be so beautiful/handsome?

※

Your Grade-schooler:

What does it mean to be truly rich?

※

Your Teenager:

Who is your favorite teacher?

Great questions to ask—

Your Preschooler:

What is the difference between a
banana and an orange?

❖

Your Grade-schooler:

What makes a house a home?

❖

Your Teenager:

Are you most like Mom or Dad?

**Conversation
Starters**

Great questions to ask—

Your Preschooler:

Would you rather draw a picture or
color one in a coloring book?

Your Grade-schooler:

What day of the week is usually your favorite?

Your Teenager:

What are the three most helpful suggestions
anyone has ever shared with you?

fun·tastic

Conversation Starters

A lot *more* great questions . . .

Children are to be seen *and* heard,
contrary to the old adage. As God's children,
we pray because we are assured by the
promises in the Bible that God will listen to us
and answer. If our Heavenly Father promises
His active attention to our concerns and
requests, as earthly fathers and mothers,
we need to be just as quick to listen to our
children. You will enjoy life's journey more
when you truly learn to talk to your kids—
and the dividends are eternal!

Conversation Starters

How effective are you at listening to your child?
Remember, the greatest question is a waste of
energy if not accompanied by a listening ear.
The following questions will assist you in getting a
sense of how in touch you are with your child:

What is on your child's mind this week?
What is your child currently most excited about?
What is currently your child's favorite music group?
. . . book? . . . movie? . . . game? . . . cartoon?
What talents or hobbies is your child most interested in?
What are your child's friends like?
What school subjects does your child most enjoy?
What experiences in your child's life have been
the most encouraging?

fun·tastic

Conversation Starters

Great listeners listen with their hearts, not just their ears. They connect with the feelings being conveyed by the other person. They refrain from abruptly interjecting their own similar experiences or struggles. They are determined to keep the focus on the speaker, not themselves.

Great listeners assume nothing—they ask.
They periodically give signals, verbally or
nonverbally, that they're following along.
They fully face the person who's talking.
"If the speaker is little," say Gary Smalley and
John Trent (as quoted in Stu Weber's book
titled *Along the Road to Manhood*),
"it may mean getting down on your knees.
Just imagine yourself five-foot-five, living in a
world populated by nine-foot giants. It gets
tiresome craning your neck all the time!"

When a parent listens actively, a child feels:
significant, enthusiastic, encouraged,
connected, important, loved, secure,
that the parent cares, and motivated
to listen to the parent in return.

fun·tastic

Conversation Starters

Choosing to listen actively to
our children when they are eager to talk
teaches them conversational skills and
strengthens them as individuals.
Open and loving dialogue can fill a child's
soul with confidence and security.

fun·tastic Conversation Starters

Your child knows you're listening when:

- your eyes focus on them;
- you turn off the TV or radio;
- you let them finish their sentences;
- you put down your newspaper or magazine;
- you ask follow-up questions;
- you don't slouch or fold your arms;
- you don't glance at your watch or a clock;
- you don't allow noise distractions to compete with their effort to talk to you.

Children are tough to fool.
They tune in to our expressions, emotions,
countenance, and general tone. As a result
of their tender spirits, our children can tell
when we're giving them our attention.

fun·tastic

Conversation Starters

Learn to listen.
Children need to be seen, to be heard,
and to be led gently. Be prepared to
absorb what your kids have to say after
you ask your questions. Listening to
their answers is the best part of asking.

He who answers before listening—

that is his folly and his shame.

Proverbs 18:13

Conversation Starters

Every waking hour is full of opportunities to cultivate closeness with our children and draw from them their insights, observations, joys, and doubts. Make the most of them. Marshall the questions. Engage their tender souls.

fun·tastic

Conversation Starters

During the ride home from church and at Sunday dinner, go ahead and dig a bit deeper into what your kids absorbed in church or Sunday school. Are there any unanswered questions? Are your children perplexed about anything that was said? This is the time to clear up any misunderstandings.

Thunderstorms filled most of my South Carolina summers growing up. When the thunder started, my mom would turn off all the lights and appliances, then sit with us on the couch. We'd listen carefully to the claps of thunder, watch the bolts of lightning, and hear the rain beating on our roof. In those awe-inspiring moments, Mom would wisely ask soul-opening questions: *Isn't God powerful? Can you imagine how strong and mighty He is? Who do you think places the lightning in the sky and sounds the thunder?* It was in those moments that I became deeply impressed with the power and majesty of my mother's God.

Conversation Starters

Another great way to keep a family close and strong is to take time for a family meeting once a week. This is a good opportunity for family devotions and talking about what's really important in life. Start when they're young. Adopt creative methods of teaching them eternal principles from the Bible. Impromptu dramas, question-and-answer sessions, music, and hands-on projects can illustrate truth and enhance the sense of adventure.

fun·tastic

Conversation Starters

Take your son or daughter on a "date." It doesn't have to be expensive to make a big impact. Ask your child in advance; set a time you'll arrive at home or school; then go out for a milk shake and a hamburger at a fast-food place. Use the setting to check in with your child. Talk about kid stuff. Ask some great questions. I've often received enthusiastic hugs in return.

Everybody likes to receive notes and letters. One way to give your children a chance to think about their answers is to ask questions in letter form. Put a note in their lunch boxes, tape one to the bathroom mirror, or send it to them in the mail. Few efforts will express your love and interest as much.

Conversation Starters

There are few times during the day when kids are more receptive than at bedtime. Make time to ask your kids questions they can think about as they drift off to sleep.

fun·tastic

Conversation Starters

Consider how much time during
the week you spend alone with your
kids in the car. What better time
for asking great questions! You have
a captive audience.

One of our favorite games to play
at the table begins with my asking a
question such as, "Okay, Kara, what were
you doing at eleven o'clock this morning?"
Kara fills us in, and then it is her turn to
pick someone else at the table and ask
the same question, inserting whatever
time she chooses. This activity never fails
to serve up some lively discussion and
help us reconnect as a family.

Conversation Starters

A parent's world is uniquely structured to provide golden opportunities for asking their kids questions. For generations, the dinner table has been the nucleus of the household, where busy lives slow down for an hour and reconnect under the love and leadership of a mother and father. Times have changed. Families eat in front of the television, or as kids get older, everyone eats at different times. But consistent meals together at the table are worth fighting for; it's a time when questions can flourish.

fun·tastic

Conversation Starters

Cultivate moments with your kids.
If you find the conversation with your
teen or preteen has suddenly left the
baby pool and dived into deeper waters,
don't be too quick to swim to the
shallow end. Chances are, the subject
has surfaced because your child
needs to talk about it.

As adults we can be just a bit
too dignified. Learn to laugh. Be silly
with your kids. See things from their
viewpoint. Remember, a preschooler's
world is only three feet tall. Be vulnerable
and allow your kids to laugh with you—
even at you. You'll create moments
you will always remember.

**Conversation
Starters**

Sometimes one of the best ways
for parents to enhance conversations
with their children is to *lighten up!*
Children's lives can quickly fill with
schedules, deadlines, and other people's
expectations and requirements.
There are moments when what they
need most from us is grace.

fun·tastic

Conversation Starters

Construct a moment with your child. Sometimes moments can be made. One great way to do this is to take this book with you as you tuck your kids into bed at night. Let a question be their last impression of the day. Your relationship with them will be warmed and strengthened. Hopefully, you'll strike up a memorable conversation.

Sometimes moments make themselves. They come unexpectedly and stare us right in the face, literally ripe with opportunity. This is where having a ready arsenal of great questions is crucial. Regardless of the topic, sharp-edged questions can turn a good moment into a great one. The following are worth committing to memory, because they will work in almost any situation:

"What can I do to help?"
"What has to be done?"
"What is your reason for asking?"
"How does that make you feel?"

Seize the moment.

Life is full of moments—
moments made and moments missed.
We can't force poignant moments with
our children. However, we can increase the
chances they will occur and make the
most of them when they do.

Conversation Starters

Wait for an answer.
Let your kids gather their thoughts
and answer before you move
on to something else.

Don't just ask questions; really listen to the answers. It never ceases to amaze me how tuned-in kids are to body language and listening skills. They seem to know whether their answer is being endured, ignored, or enjoyed.

Conversation Starters

Remember, questions beget questions.
Once you're in the front door of a young
person's mind, there is a house full of furniture
and people to discover. Use follow-up questions
to discover more about feelings and opinions.
Here are some examples:

"How long have you felt this way?"
"How does that make you feel?"
"What do you think about that?"
"How does that affect you?"
"How did you come to that conclusion?"

fun·tastic

Conversation Starters

Use the word "if" a lot. For instance, you could ask "If you could have any job in the world, which one would you choose?" Or, "If you could visit anyplace on the planet, where would you go?" Or, "If you could change anything about yourself, what would it be?" "If" questions are powerful tools for tapping the imagination.

72

Simply plowing through a litany of questions will make a child, especially an older one, feel more like an interviewee than a son or daughter. Questions are a seasoning that should fill every great conversation. They should be mixed with advice, encouragement, information, lots of listening, and humor.

Conversation Starters

Inquire, but don't interrogate. If your kids perceive you as a prosecutor, trying to lead them to your desired conclusion, they will quickly retreat behind a wall of silence. Before asking a question, stop and ask yourself:

What attitude is motivating my question? Am I asking in order to discover or to deride? Does my question sound accusatory or merely inquisitive? Would I want to be asked this question by someone in authority over me?

fun·tastic

Conversation Starters

Here is a set of steps that begins with lighter fare
and moves progressively deeper. Ask about:

Favorites—Find out the kind of sports teams, cereal, music, and
movies your child loves.

Fun—Discover something your child genuinely enjoys.

Friends—Every child needs help sorting out relationships and
how they work.

Feelings—Check the temperature of your child's soul to show
love and concern.

Failures—Parental patience is necessary when your children
stumble and struggle through life.

Fears—Find out about the things that hurt or haunt your children.

The Future—From their earliest years, children need to be asked
about their dreams, hopes, and aspirations.

Faith—Parents need to nurture and challenge their children
toward spiritual growth.

66

Our kids are naturally primed to talk about movies, music, sports, and hobbies. However, sometimes they need most to talk about their feelings, their friendships, and their dreams. The wise parent learns to carefully navigate a conversation from the trivial to the important, from matters of the mind to matters of the heart. Go below the "waterline." In other words, dig underneath the trivial and open the soul.

Conversation Starters

Be precise when asking questions.
I can't count how many times I've been asked,
"What do you think is God's will for your life?"
I've always found that question too broad for me to
tackle. But I will never forget the time someone
asked me the same question in a different way:
"If you could do anything you wanted to do for the
kingdom of God and be guaranteed it would
succeed, what would you do?" Now that is one
excitingly specific question. It dug deep and
drew out the dreams within me.

fun·tastic

Conversation Starters

Ask questions that cannot be
answered with a mere "yes" or "no."
Don't just ask for an opinion;
ask for a reason for the opinion.

On America's frontier during the nineteenth century, Quaker families collectively developed four great questions that were regularly used in small groups to get acquainted with newly arriving settlers. It is obvious that these questions were carefully, if not prayerfully, constructed. They were so effective that some small groups still use them today; there is a flow to this set of questions that creates openness. They move from general to personal, from above the "waterline" to below, without threatening anyone:

"When you were ten years old, how was your house heated?"
"What was the warmest room in your house?"
"Who were you closest to?"
"When did God become more than just a name to you?"

Conversation Starters

Closed questions are those that can be handled briefly: "Yes," "No," "Good," "Bad," or "Okay." For example, a closed question would be, "How are you doing?"

On the other hand, open questions draw on your child's imagination or genuine feelings. For example, "If you had to describe how you're feeling as a weather report, would you say you're feeling sunny, cloudy, partly sunny, or partly cloudy? What do you think is making you feel that way?"

fun·tastic

Conversation Starters

If you've ever asked someone, "So, how was your day?" and gotten a mumbled "okay" in reply, you know that some questions work better than others. What is the difference between a great question and a dead-end question? A great question elicits a full response.

God only knows the potential,
the ideas, the dreams, and the hopes
wrapped up in the soul of a child.
Parents get to nudge open those souls
and watch them emerge as individuals
made in God's image. Questions are
the essential tools in this process.

Conversation Starters

Questions are education in the truest sense of the word. Education comes from the Latin word *educare,* which means "to draw forth." Most of us do too much stuffing things in and not enough drawing things forth. Instead of saying, "Well, that's what you get!" we need to say, "Oh, that's interesting. What happened? How do you feel?" or "What did you learn from it?"

fun·tastic

Conversation Starters

Questions bring your child's dreams and desires close enough to the surface for you to affirm and encourage them. Whom does your daughter most admire? What heroes does your son often think about? What are their highest hopes and greatest aspirations? Just ask!

Questions clarify what the child actually had in mind. They keep us from jumping to false conclusions.

Conversation Starters

Questions cultivate intimacy between parent and child. Considerate questions draw children closer. These questions slow us down in our much-too-busy lifestyles and build bridges of interest that bond us even closer with our children.

fun·tastic

Conversation Starters

Questions inspire your child to
establish values and standards for living.
Jesus used questions powerfully to
challenge His followers. In fact,
He interspersed no fewer than fourteen
questions in His Sermon on the Mount.

One of the greatest teachers of all time was Socrates, who lived in Athens from 470 to 399 B.C. He taught Plato, who taught Aristotle, who taught Alexander the Great. Socrates' reputation in the fifth-century B.C. as the wisest man in the world was based upon his own claim that among all men, he was the most aware of his own ignorance, thereby making him the wisest! His method of teaching depended on asking his students questions, hoping by this means to open their minds and drive them to a deeper consideration of the issues.

D. Bruce Lockerbie
Asking Questions

Questions often create a sense
of need within your child for principles
and insights that you are uniquely equipped
to teach. Great questions can evoke a topic
that's truly important. Create or discover a
hunger for wisdom within your child
by using great questions.

Conversation Starters

Questions help you discern your child's true emotional and spiritual needs. By asking questions, a parent can tune into what a child's greatest needs are *today,* as opposed to yesterday or a month ago.

Questions bring focus to the time you spend with your children. Instead of wasting the hours, seize spontaneous moments while you're driving them to school, tucking them into bed at night, standing in line at the checkout stand, or during half-time at a football game. These can be just as fruitful as the organized "quality times" you plan.

Conversation Starters

The "What Would You Do If...?" game is a great exercise to play with your child. For example: "What if you were taking a test, and the teacher walked out of the room? Let's say you were sitting next to the smartest kid in the class and you could easily see his answers. What would you do?" The response to such a question may tell you a lot about your child's moral development.

fun·tastic

Conversation Starters

Questions show you how much
of your parental training is taking root.
We spend so much time pouring
knowledge and wisdom into our
children's lives that it makes sense to see
if they're actually absorbing any of it.

Questions model good social skills
for your child. Children, teenagers, and
adults alike are better prepared to face life
if they know how to ask good questions.
Parents who ask their children great
questions strengthen the relational skills
of their kids, assuring them greater
success in social situations.

Conversation Starters

Questions assure your children
that you really care about their thoughts
and feelings. We tend to trust people who
are tuned in to our needs and respect us
enough to hold those sacred trusts in
confidence. Parents have an unparalleled
opportunity to do both.

fun·tastic

Conversation Starters

Questions show your genuine interest in your child. Merely saying, "I love you" or "I really care about you" is not enough. When parents care enough to frame a well-suited question and patiently tap into what may interest or concern their child, they open more than a conversation. They open a soul.

Salesmen ask questions because they want to make a sale. Teachers ask questions because they want to open minds. Police detectives ask questions because they want to solve crimes. Parents ask questions because they love their children.

**Conversation
Starters**

Parenting at its best is much more than
getting children through school, teaching
them responsibility, and raising them to be
law-abiding citizens. Parenting is about
opening a soul, freeing a spirit, and
unleashing a life brimming with potential to
discover all God has intended for them.

fun·tastic

Conversation Starters

Having children and not asking
them questions is like owning an easel
and never painting a picture.
The best a child has to offer may only
be a question away.

As clearly as an invitation beckons
a friend to attend a birthday party,
football game, or backyard barbecue,
questions invite children in by evoking
a response. Questions engage them.
Effectively formed and sensitively placed,
questions construct an atmosphere of
interest that draws upon the hidden
resources and needs of the soul.

Ambassadors use questions to build bridges
between countries that are oceans apart.
Teachers use questions to build bridges between
themselves and their students. Spouses use questions
to build intimacy with each other. Managers use
questions to cultivate teamwork and productivity
among employees. Wise parents use questions to
bridge the generation divide with their children,
whether en route to nursery school or on the
way home from a high-school soccer game.

fun·tastic

Conversation Starters

You cannot visit the Bible's paramount parenting passages of Deuteronomy 6 or Ephesians 6 without learning that parenting involves imparting. You'll read there about impressing, loving, training, encouraging, and comforting your children. However, parenting also involves drawing out the heart of your child. A great question depends upon openness, honesty, cooperation, and friendship. King Solomon put it this way: "The purposes of a man's heart are deep waters, but a man of understanding draws them out" (Proverbs 20:5).

If you're like most people,
it's easy to get stuck telling your kids
what to do, how to do it, and when to
do it, instead of taking time to ask
meaningful questions. To most of us,
parenting involves telling, not asking,
but it doesn't have to be that way.

Conversation Starters

Questions are one of the most
effective, yet perhaps, most underused
tools in a parent's toolbox. Just spending
five minutes expressing a personal interest
in your child will do more to build your
relationship than five months of trying
to get that child interested in you.

fun·tastic

Conversation Starters

Art Linkletter captured the hearts of millions thirty-five years ago when he tried something on television that no one else was doing—asking children questions. He carved out a niche for himself and fascinated his audience by giving children the microphone while the adults sat back and listened.

Linkletter summed up his motivation in his book *Kids Say the Darnedest Things:* "There's a vast gulf between the world of children and our own. And every time we bridge that gulf—even if it's only for a moment—we recapture some of the freshness and spontaneity that makes life worth living."